Jesus saves!

Jesus Saves the Day!
Hip Hip, Hooray!

Written by
C.C. Strachan

Illustrated by
Chernelle Walkes

ISBN-13: 978-0692460672

ACKNOWLEDGMENTS

To my wonderful family and friends for your continued support;
and to CanStockPhoto http://www.canstockphoto.com/ for your creative clip art images.

What do grown-ups mean
and why do they beam;
when they say, "Jesus saves!"?
Is it because He's super brave?

To know why Jesus saves,
you need to know what God gave.
So answer me these,
four questions please.

**Would you give your only toy
to a mean and angry little boy?**

**And would you perform a good deed
to a friend always in need?**

**Would you still play a game
with a friend that said you are lame?**

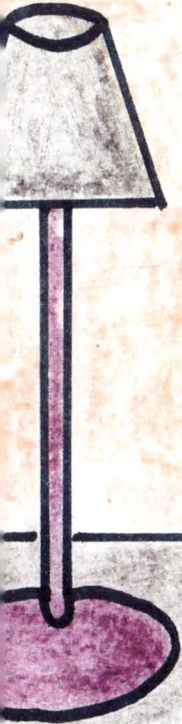

And if someone said "I don't like you," would you still like them too?

This is what God gave to us
and He didn't make a fuss.
He gave His one and only son, (John 3:16)
to mean and angry persons.

For God so loved the world that he gave his one and only Son, that whoever believes in him shall not perish but have eternal life. (John 3:16)

He even shares his sun and rain with those that call him ugly names. (Mat 5:45)

But I tell you, love your enemies and pray for those who persecute you, that you may be children of your Father in heaven. He causes his sun to rise on the evil and the good, and sends rain on the righteous and the unrighteous. (Mat 5:44-45)

No one knows
why God loves us so!
For His love has no end
and He calls us friend.

For if it were not for Him,
then things would be grim.
We would all go astray,
living life our own way.

Like a boy left alone in the park,
we would all be lost, alone in the dark.

But wait! This is not our story,
because God showed his glory.

For God needed a plan,
that would save man.
He knew his people must be saved
and needed someone help them behave.

For God so loved us,
that He gave us Jesus.
That whoever believes in Him;
will spend forever with Him. (John 3.16).

This is why people beam
and even shout and scream:
"Jesus saves the day,
hip hip, hooray!"

Dear Jesus,

Thank you for Calvary,
and what you did for me.
For you died on a cross
to save that which was lost. (Luke 19:10)
You thought of me
so that I can be free,
to love our heavenly Father;
who sent you to gather
his people to draw near,
just because He cares.
So Lord I ask you today.
To come into my heart and stay
and show me your way.
O Lord, I pray.
Amen!

ABOUT THE AUTHOR

C. C. Strachan has been a Christian for over fifteen years and lives in Brooklyn, New York, with her Evangelist husband and their four-year-old son. She holds a master's degree in financial engineering and has worked in the financial industry for over fifteen years; she's presently pursuing an additional master's degree in Christian apologetics from Biola University. C.C. Strachan and her husband are the founders of Power of Worship Ministries, Inc., a nonprofit organization that provides food for the homeless.

Is God My Imaginary Friend?

Is God Real?

Written By:
C.C Strachan

Illustrated By: Chernelle Walkes

Look for other C.C. Strachan books at:
www.childrenbooksaboutgod.com

www.ingramcontent.com/pod-product-compliance
Lightning Source LLC
Chambersburg PA
CBHW041238040426
42445CB00004B/72

9780692460672